FREEDOM FORCES

★ U.S. MARINES ★
RAPID RESPONSE FORCE

Tom Greve

Rourke
Educational Media
rourkeeducationalmedia.com

www.rourkeeducationalmedia.com

PHOTO CREDITS: Cover photo: marines photo by Lance Cpl. Anne K. Henry, cover and title page metal border © Eky Studio; back cover and title page: flag © SFerdon; Pages 4/5 main photo marines.mil photographer: Lance Cpl. Pete Sanders, inset photo army.mil; page 6 photos courtesy U.S. military photographers Gunnery Sergeant Demetrio Espinosa and Lt. Ken Shade; page 7 photos courtesy U.S. military, photo by EDDIE MCCROSSAN, courtesy U.S. Navy photo by Mass Communication Specialist Seaman Joseph Pol Sebastian Gocong, courtesy U.S. Marines photo by SGT Anthony Ortiz, courtesy U.S. Air Force photo by © Senior Airman Gustavo Gonzalez, bottom photo © Pfc. Lora Harter; page 8 photo by PFC Charlie Chavez; pages 9, 10, 11 courtesy US Marine Corps; pages 12/13 and 14 courtesy National Archives and Records Administration; page 15 National Archives and U.S. Military; pages 16/17 © The Associated Press /Joe Rosenthal; page 17 courtesy U.S. Marines; Pages 18/19 courtesy U.S. Navy and U.S. Marines; page 20 courtesy National Archives and Records Administration; page 21 courtesy U.S. Marines; page 22 © UpstateNYer; page 23 courtesy U.S. Marines, photo by Lance Cpl. Tyler Reiriz, map © Pjasha; pages 24-26 courtesy U.S. Marines; page 27 portrait of John A. Lejeune courtesy U.S. Marines, plaque of John A. Lejeune © Leonard J. DeFrancisci; page 28 courtesy National Archives and Records Administration; page 29 courtesy U.S. Marines

Edited by Precious McKenzie

Designed and Produced by Blue Door Publishing, FL

Library of Congress Cataloging-in-Publication Data

Greve. Tom.
   U.S. Marines: Rapid Response Force / Tom Greve
   p. cm. -- (Freedom Forces)
   ISBN 978-1-62169-922-4 (hard cover) (alk. paper)
   ISBN 978-1-62169-817-3 (soft cover)
   ISBN 978-1-62717-026-0 (e-book)
   Library of Congress Control Number: 2013938874

Also Available as:
ROURKE'S
e-Books

Rourke Educational Media
Printed in the United States of America,
North Mankato, Minnesota

Rourke
Educational Media

rourkeeducationalmedia.com

customerservice@rourkeeducationalmedia.com
PO Box 643328 Vero Beach, Florida 32964

TABLE OF CONTENTS

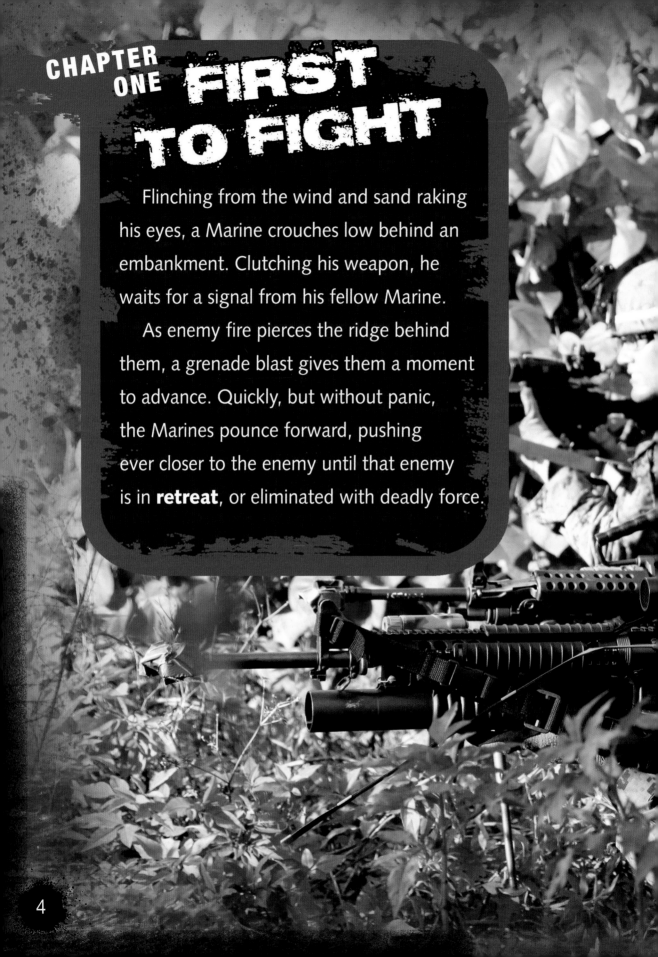

CHAPTER ONE

FIRST TO FIGHT

Flinching from the wind and sand raking his eyes, a Marine crouches low behind an embankment. Clutching his weapon, he waits for a signal from his fellow Marine.

As enemy fire pierces the ridge behind them, a grenade blast gives them a moment to advance. Quickly, but without panic, the Marines pounce forward, pushing ever closer to the enemy until that enemy is in **retreat**, or eliminated with deadly force.

U.S. Marines are an amphibious force, meaning they can attack by land or sea. They have been at the forefront of nearly every major battle in the nation's history.

The United States has the world's largest military force. The Army, Navy, Air Force, Marines, Coast Guard, and Central Intelligence Agency all play roles in defending the country against forces that would aim to harm the nation, its people, or its resources.

The Marine Corps is the smallest of the four major **combat** service branches. The Corps operates in tandem with the U.S. Navy, although the two have different roles in defending the U.S.

America's 9-1-1 Force.

Like a person calling 9-1-1 in an emergency, so too does the U.S. government call on the Marines. Smaller in number than the Army, Navy, or Air Force, the Marines are the most rapid responders of all the military branches. With transportation support from the Navy, the Marine Corps prides itself on being able to respond to any crisis on Earth within 6 hours.

Basic Roles of U.S. Military Branches in Combat

Army: Ground combat operations. Maintenance and support of land-based weapons.

Air Force: Air combat operations. Maintenance and support of military planes and helicopters.

Navy: Combat operations at sea. Maintenance and support of sea-going vessels and weapons, such as ships and submarines.

Marines: Amphibious combat force. Using support from the Navy, attack enemy from the air or water. Establish operation for advancing combat on land.

FREEDOM FACT

The U.S. Marine Corps lives by the motto *Semper Fi*, Latin for always faithful.

The Corps relies on a specific chain of command to streamline nearly everything it does. There is little tolerance for individual or selfish action. All members operate according to a code of conduct. This means Marines follow orders from superiors without question. Marines operate this way in peacetime as well as during times of war.

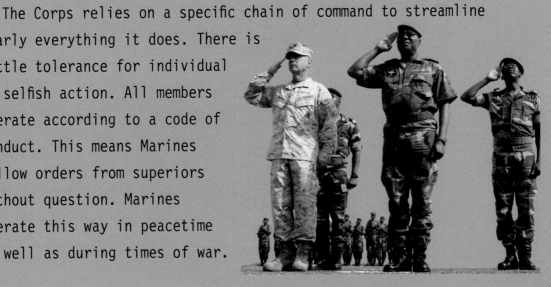

Marines are an especially tough, multi-skilled fighting force within the U.S. military. Marine Boot Camp is the toughest basic training program of the major military branches. Marine recruits have to be able to swim, as well as demonstrate strength and endurance. They also have to learn and memorize a great deal of information quickly. As part of a rapid response amphibious force, Marines must be fit and ready for action at all times.

Where Marines are Made

All Marines attend a 72-day boot camp at either Parris Island in South Carolina, or San Diego, California. The training is the same at both places, extremely tough! Many Marines say the 72 days spent at either of these training grounds are the most difficult 10 weeks of their lives.

Women and the Marine Corps

Women are a valuable part of the U.S. Marine Corps. They may be on the verge of expanding their role. They have traditionally filled support roles like language interpreters or medical staff. However, as of 2013, women can serve in combat roles as long as they pass the physical test during training. Women currently make up about 7 percent of the roughly 200,000 active Marines in the Corps. Overall, women make up about 14 percent of the 1.4 million people serving in the U.S. armed forces.

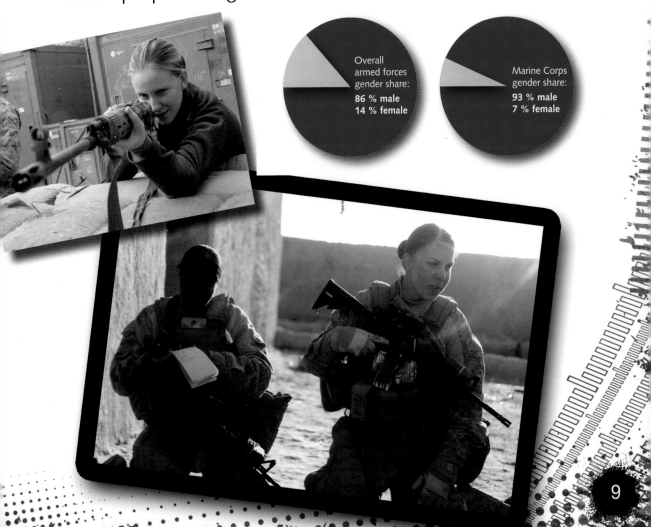

Overall armed forces gender share:
86 % male
14 % female

Marine Corps gender share:
93 % male
7 % female

CHAPTER TWO

MARINE CORPS HISTORY:

PROJECTING POWER FROM THE SEA

The United States Marine Corps is as old as the nation itself. Its creation, during preparations for the Revolutionary War, came from the need to have men fight from ships and advance onto land against British Forces.

FREEDOM FACT

Birth of the Corps:
On November 10, 1775, at a meeting of the Continental Congress at Tun's Tavern in Philadelphia, Pennsylvania, formal plans were made to assemble two battalions of Continental Marines. To this day, Marines celebrate November 10 as the birthday of the U.S. Marine Corps.

Another name for a Marine is Leatherneck, a reference to the stiff collars on their uniforms. The collars were originally made of leather.

After winning independence from Britain, the newly formed United States maintained its Navy and its Marine battalions. During the 1800s, American merchant ships often encountered thieves and were attacked by pirates while at sea. The Marines traveled with the Navy, defending these vessels and enforcing their safe passage.

Marine of Merit

In 1912, First Lieutenant Alfred Cunningham became the first Marine in flight when he took naval aviation training. Other Marines soon followed and, by the time the U.S. entered World War I in 1917, the Marines could attack by land, sea, or air.

First Lieutenant Alfred Cunningham
1881-1939

As advances in ship design and weapons technology expanded the capabilities of the U.S. Navy, the amphibious skills of Marines became even more important to military combat strategy.

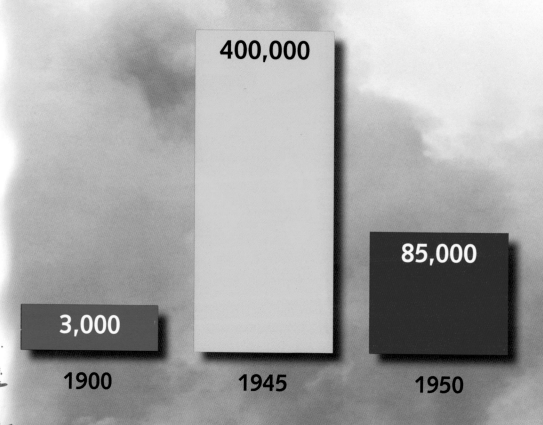

The Marine Corps and the overall U.S. Military grew immensely between 1900 and the end of World War II in 1945. There were 3,000 active duty Marines in the Corps as of 1900, but more than 400,000 by 1945. The Corps reduced its size sharply again once the war was over.

The history of the United States, its military, and the Marine Corps changed forever on December 7, 1941. It was on this day that Japanese fighter planes bombed the U.S. military base at Pearl Harbor, Hawaii. The air raid left more than 2,400 Americans dead and launched the United States fully into World War II.

The attack on Pearl Harbor set into motion the largest military action in the nation's history, and put the Marines front and center in a worldwide fight against Japan and Germany.

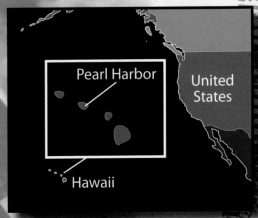

CHAPTER THREE

AMPHIBIOUS FIGHTING in WORLD WAR II

World War II involved massive U.S. military operations in Europe and Africa against Germany, and throughout the Pacific Ocean against the Japanese. As usual, whether on land or at sea, the Marine Corps was ready for the fight.

The Marines made heavy use of an invention called the Higgins boat during World War II. Named after the New Orleans shipbuilder who designed it, the boats carried Marines from anchored ships to dry land to begin their assault.

Much of the fighting in the Pacific **theater** was at sea and on islands. The amphibious attack skills of the Marines were tailor-made for some of the war's most intense battles.

Marines of Merit

While the country was growing more **desegregated**, so was the Marine Corps. In 1942, with World War II raging, the Corps recruited its first African-Americans, and by the end of the decade, there would be nearly 20,000 African-American Marines. Native American Marines also played important roles during World War II. Known as code-talkers, they sent and received U.S. radio messages in their Navajo language. If enemies intercepted the messages, they could not decipher the language. This helped keep American forces safe.

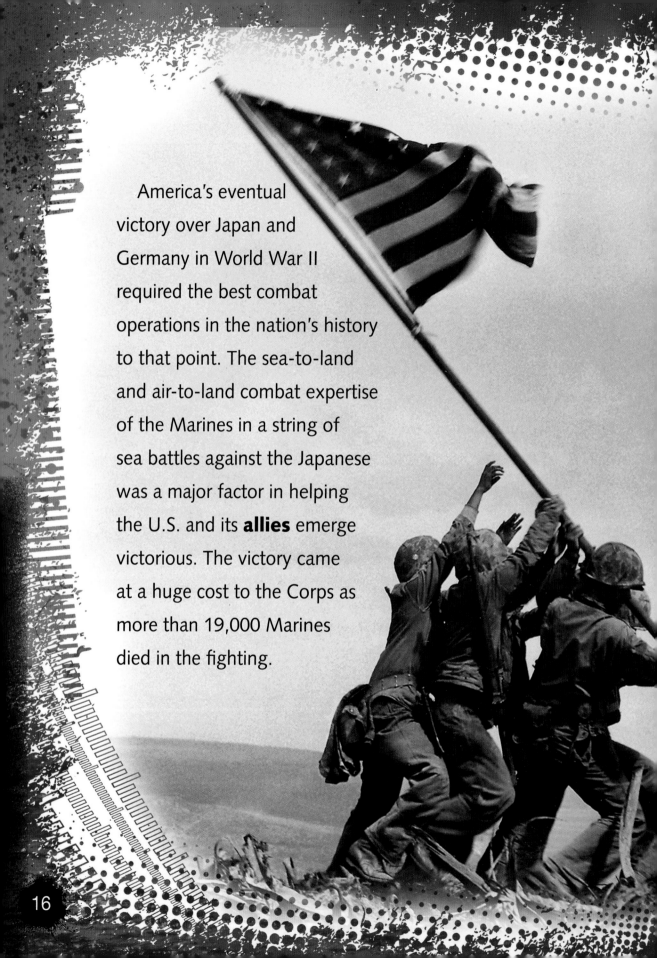

America's eventual victory over Japan and Germany in World War II required the best combat operations in the nation's history to that point. The sea-to-land and air-to-land combat expertise of the Marines in a string of sea battles against the Japanese was a major factor in helping the U.S. and its **allies** emerge victorious. The victory came at a huge cost to the Corps as more than 19,000 Marines died in the fighting.

Marine of Merit

Lewis Puller, nicknamed Chesty, earned more combat service medals and honors than any Marine in history. His heroism in the pivotal World War II battle of Guadalcanal not only saved the lives of many of his fellow Marines, but also helped defeat the Japanese Navy. He died in 1971. To this day, Marines in boot camp often end their day reciting the slogan "Goodnight Chesty Puller, wherever you are!"

Lewis Puller
1898-1971

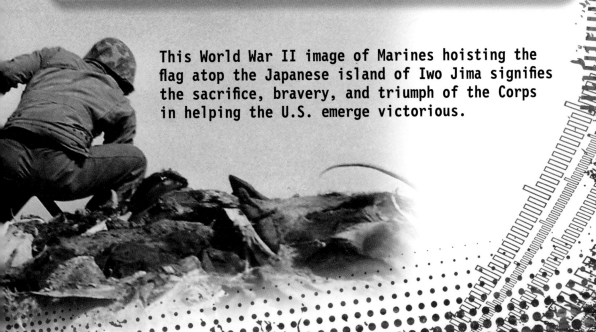

This World War II image of Marines hoisting the flag atop the Japanese island of Iwo Jima signifies the sacrifice, bravery, and triumph of the Corps in helping the U.S. emerge victorious.

Since World War II, the nature of military combat has become more complicated. Not just in terms of battlefields and equipment, but also in terms of the United States' enemies and their fighting tactics. Through it all, the Marines have adjusted, always first to fight.

Part of what makes Marines so capable in combat is the strict rifle marksmanship training they take during boot camp.

Draft vs Volunteer

From World War I through the Vietnam War, the U.S. used drafts to build up the staffing of its military during wartime. That meant all young men could be picked for mandatory service in the country's armed forces. Since 1973, men and women volunteer to serve, including in the U.S. Marines.

If World War II was a triumph of the U.S. military, the Vietnam War may have been a cautionary tale. Fighting valiantly against an often hidden and secretive enemy in the Asian jungles, the U.S. Army and the Marines in particular, spent a decade stuck in a difficult struggle between North and South Vietnam.

The Vietnam War

Vietnam was among the deadliest military conflicts in the history of the Marine Corps. Between 1965 and 1975, more than 13,000 Marines died in combat in Vietnam. The war created widespread and sometimes violent disagreement among the American people and the U.S. government over the proper role of the U.S. military in foreign affairs. Those arguments continue to this very day.

CHAPTER FOUR

RAPID RESPONSE TO TERRORISM AND TRAGEDY

Perhaps no single event affected the U.S. Marine Corps or the U.S. military, in general, more than the **terrorist** attacks of September 11th, 2001.

The attack involved **hijacking** commercial airplanes and crashing them into places like New York City's World Trade Center and the Pentagon building in Washington D.C. Nearly 3,000 people died, most of them at the World Trade Center.

The terrorists flew hijacked jets into each of the 110-story towers of the World Trade Center. Both buildings were destroyed.

Unlike Pearl Harbor, which was an act of war committed by another country's military, September 11 was the work of hidden and secretive terrorists. In the years since the attacks, the Marines have been in two major conflicts overseas. First, the U.S. invaded Afghanistan to wage war on suspected terrorist groups involved in the planning of the 9/11 attacks.

The War in Afghanistan continues in 2013. The U.S. also invaded Iraq in 2003. Although U.S. combat operations stopped in Iraq in 2010, Marines have spearheaded the U.S. effort in each theater of operation.

During the wars in Iraq and Afghanistan, the Marine Corps has increasingly worked as partners with local police and civilians to identify those working in secret against the U.S. The military calls this work counterinsurgency. Since Vietnam, and especially in both Iraq and Afghanistan, this has become a major part of the Marines' combat mission.

As efficient as the Marines' rapid response force is when heading into combat, it is also valuable in responding to noncombat **humanitarian** emergencies.

When Hurricane Katrina flooded New Orleans, Louisiana in 2005, the Marines moved in to help rescue people stranded by the water. When an earthquake devastated the island nation of Haiti in 2010, the U.S. sent thousands of Marines to help survivors and maintain order amid the wreckage.

Some Marines test into the elite Special Operations Command sector of the Corps. MARSOC, or Marines Special Operation Command, represents the best of the best. Already toughened by the rigors of life in the Corps, these Marines undergo even more intense and specialized training for harsh and often secret combat challenges. Special Operation Commands has grown across all military branches in response to the threat of terrorism.

WHAT'S IN A NAME?

The term *soldier* does not technically apply to Marines. A Marine is just that: a Marine. The Army has soldiers, the Navy has sailors, the Air Force has airmen. It may seem technical, but it matters. They are Marines.

25

The modern Marine Corps is a big part of why the U.S. military is the most capable national defense organization the world has ever seen.

The head of the United State Marine Corps is called the General Commandant. James Amos is the 35th in the history of the Marine Corps. As Commandant, he is the highest ranking person in the entire Corps. The Commandant is also a member of the Joint Chiefs of Staff, which advises the President on military matters.

General Commandant James Amos 1946-

Always faithful and first to fight, U.S. Marines live by a code of honor. They train and prepare. They follow orders from their superiors. If called upon by the president, they can respond to any crisis by air, sea, or land.

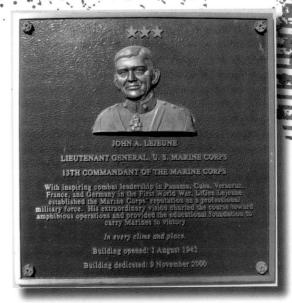

**Camp Lejeune
"Home of Expeditionary
Forces in Readiness."**

Marines call John Lejeune the greatest of all Leathernecks. He spent more than 40 years serving in the Corps in a variety of combat roles. From 1920 until 1929, he served as General Commandant. Today, North Carolina's Camp Lejeune, the main base of all Marine Corps operations, is named in his honor.

Marine of Merit
*Commandant
John Lejeune*
1867-1942

TIMELINE

World War I (1917-1920)
1918:
Marines prevail in the war's bloodiest battle, defeating German forces at the Battle of Belleau Woods, France.

World War II (1941-1945)
1942:
Newly designed Higgins boats help Marines attack beaches against Japanese forces at Guadalcanal Island.

Korean War (1950-1953)
1950:
Jet engines begin outnumbering propeller aircraft among Marine fleet, increasing speed of air transport and combat.

1920:
Marine aviation is used in combat for the first time.

1945:
Marines capture Japanese Island of Iwo Jima as U.S. gains upper hand in Pacific theater and the war overall.

1951:
Helicopters first used to land Marines into combat.

1952:
Marines begin wearing lightweight, bulletproof vests in combat.

1975:
Marines rescue last Americans from embassy in Saigon before it falls to Communism.

2006:
Marine Corps adopts new counterinsurgency field manual to guide efforts in Iraq and Afghanistan.

Vietnam War (1965-1975)
1965:
Marines begin counterinsurgency patrols.

Gulf War in Iraq (1991)

War in Iraq (2003-2010)

2002:
MARPAT, or Marine Pattern camouflage, avoids detection from the naked eye as well as digital lenses.

War in Afghanistan (2001-present)
2013:
Marines extend use of K-MAX unmanned cargo helicopter for transport of supplies in combat via remote control.

SHOW WHAT YOU KNOW

1. Who does the Marine Corps operate in tandem with?
2. Where do all Marines attend a 72-day boot camp?
3. When was the birth of the U.S. Marine Corps?
4. What happened on December 7, 1941?
5. Who is the head of the United States Marine Corps?

GLOSSARY

allies (AL-ize): different groups joining together to
battle a common enemy

combat (KOM-bat): fighting between groups or armies

desegregated (dee-SEG-ruh-GAY-ted): allowing people
of all races to join

hijacking (HYE-jak-ing): the forceful takeover of an
airplane to change its destination

humanitarian (hyoo-MAN-uh-TAIR-ee-uhn): an organized
attempt to relieve suffering

retreat (ree-TREET): to back up, or move away from an
advancing force

terrorist (TER-uhr-ist): a person who commits acts
of violence in order to try and affect change

theater (THEE-uh-tur): a region where combat takes place

Index

Websites to Visit

www.marines.com

www.marinecorpsfamilyfoundation.org

www.marineband.usmc.mil/kids

About the Author

Tom Greve lives in Chicago. He is married, has two children, and enjoys reading and writing about military history. He has an older brother who served six years in the U.S. Navy. He is grateful to all who have served in the U.S. Military.

Meet The Author!
www.meetREMauthors.com